Say Hello Wombat

Photography Steve Parish
Words Pat Slater

Steve Parish
PUBLISHING

Mother wombat
keeps her eye
on baby wombat.

Baby wombat looks
at baby wallaby riding
in mother's pouch.

The baby wombat has great fun playing on a log.

Wombats
comb their fur
with their claws.

Wombat,
kookaburras and platypus
all meet at the creek.

Wombat meets a spiky friend.
Hello echidna!

Wombat wonders
if the kangaroos
are playing or fighting.

Wombat sneak

owards the noisy cockatoos.

A cockatoo yells loudly and frightens poor wombat away.

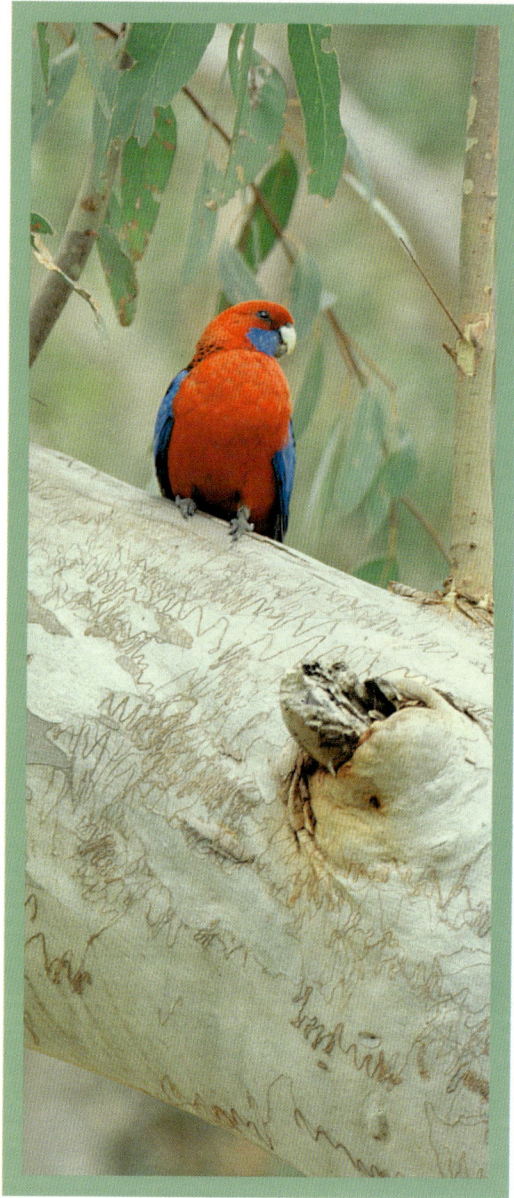

Rosella
and koala
ask
what
all the noise
is about.

The kangaroos sit up,
then hop away in fright.

Wombat and emu
eat tasty grass
together.

Wombats have soft fur and emus have soft feathers.

The kookaburras and the kangaroos know that the bush is full of secrets.

Wallabies may pass on
secrets,
but wombats never tell.